The cover photograph depicts construction of the Bergdorf Goodman Men's Store. It was taken by Burke Uzzle and appeared in *The New York Times* magazine section on August 20, 1990.

The store opened a month later.

PRAISE FOR
A Retailer's Lifetime of Lessons Learned

"Ira Neimark's latest book, *A Retailer's Lifetime of Lessons Learned*, is filled with wisdom and great advice. His many years of retail experience allow him to offer the very best guidance to all of us in the retail business. These lessons are invaluable to anyone contemplating a career in this dynamic industry."

Robert Chavez
President and CEO, Hermes USA

"Ira Neimark reveals the roadmap to success in his brilliant new book, *A Retailer's Lifetime of Lessons Learned*. It should be required reading for all who seek fame and fortune in the retail industry worldwide."

Mark A. Cohen, Professor
Columbia University
Graduate School of Business

"In *A Retailer's Lifetime of Lesson Learned*, luxury retail legend Ira Neimark brings a refreshing, thoughtful perspective to a remarkable career of over sixty years and boils it down to simple but powerful lessons learned. The book is instructive, inspiring, and filled with the humanity that is Ira. He has produced another brilliant and immensely practical book."

Savio S. Chan, President & CEO
US China Partners
Vice Chairman
Luxury Marketing Council China

"Whether you're in the IT industry, the fashion industry, or any other industry, *A Retailer's Lifetime of Lessons Learned* can be extremely helpful to you and your career. Ira Neimark is an American success story from whom anyone can gain inspiration.

He has truly inspired me, and I have made his books a 'must read' for all my employees."

Ira is a passionate storyteller, and it shows in A Retailer's Lifetime of Lessons Learned. His stories and the lessons learned conveyed in this book will inspire you to continually better yourself personally and professionally. The knowledge he has gained over his memorable career is applicable to anyone who wants to learn how to become successful."

Russell Sarder
Author of Learning and Effective Learning Methods
Chairman & CEO of NetCom Learning

"A Retailer's Lifetime of Lessons Learned is a brilliant compilation of the steps necessary to succeed in business and life. It's fast-read format, with discrete categories and, especially, the brilliant 'lessons learned' after each vignette, makes it a tremendous guide for anyone who wants to be a CEO or lead a purpose-driven life."

Robert Reiss
Host, The CEO Show
Writer for Forbes.com and co-author The Transformative CEO

"One doesn't become a legend in luxury retailing without discipline, a great eye, a solid strategic sense, an impeccable sense of style, and the ability to court, impress, and engage the best of the best. Mr. Neimark is a luxury marketer's marketer and A Retailer's Lifetime of Lessons Learned is a treasure trove for those savvy and street-wise enough to apply these lessons from a lifetime of wisdom.

A Retailer's Lifetime of Lessons Learned is a wonderful vade mecum and one of the best investments for luxury marketers who are passionate about 'sharpening the saw' of their approach to their discipline and recognize the importance of too-often-ignored fundamentals that make brands sing."

Gregory J. Furman
Founder & Chairman
The Luxury Marketing Council

A Retailer's Lifetime of Lessons Learned

Ira Neimark

Former CEO, Bergdorf Goodman

GamePlan Press, Inc.
Arlington, VA
www.gameplanpress.com

Copyright 2012 © by Ira Neimark

All rights reserved under the Pan-American and International Copyright Conventions. This book may not be reproduced in whole or in part, in any form or by any means electronic or mechanical, including photocopying, recording, or by any information storage and retrieval system now known or hereinafter invented, without written permission of the publisher, GamePlan Press Inc.

ISBN: 978-0-9882177-1-3

GamePlan Press, Inc.
910 South George Mason Drive
Arlington, VA 22204
www.gameplanpress.com

Dedicated to all the present and future young entrepreneurs looking for the keys (or Lessons Learned) to successful business careers.

Best Regards,

Ira

Acknowledgments

REFLECTING BACK ON MY long retail career, I consider myself fortunate to have had the opportunity to meet so many of the outstanding retailers of the twentieth century. I learned something from every one of them:

William M. Holmes, the president of Bonwit Teller I mention throughout the book, launched my career.

Beatrice Auerbach, the head of G. Fox & Co. whom I also mention frequently, taught me storekeeping.

Stanley Marcus was the best salesman and PR professional of them all. He was a legend, famous for promoting a relatively small store in Dallas so effectively that people thought it was more than twice its size.

Sam Walton is another legendary retailer who surprised me a few years ago when I congratulated him for receiving the NRDGA gold medal award. He replied that I should be congratulated for making Bergdorf Goodman what it is today.

Jean-Louis Dumas, the head of Hermes for many years, taught me quality. Quality, not quantity, is the name of the game in luxury retailing.

Too many to mention, needless to say, are the wonderful merchants who ran the many stores that belonged to the Frederick Atkins Buying Office. These were the merchants who were, for the better part of the twentieth century, the major independent retailers in the United States. They shaped the industry and each of them, in his or her own way, taught me the many basic principles of retailing that helped me reach my ambitious goals.

Of course I must also mention the people who, through their help and encouragement, made this book possible.

My wife Jackie, always there, encouraged me, and corrected and reshaped a good number of the pages you will read.

Hallie Seegal, my granddaughter and a recent editor at the Huffington, post recommended, as did my publisher, Maryann Karinch, that I include brief anecdotes to describe the experiences that provided my "lessons learned." My youngest granddaughter, Betsy Lewis, provided computer technical support and showed me how to easily transfer the lessons from both my published books into the new manuscript. Together, they helped make this book contemporary. Maryann's encouragement and guidance throughout make the book possible and Judith Bailey, our editor, made the book what I hoped it could be.

Finally, I want to acknowledge Professor Mark Cohen of the Columbia Business School. When I first described my idea for the book to him, he said, "This is brilliant." He is greatly responsible for what you are about to read.

Foreword

A RETAILER'S LIFETIME OF LESSONS LEARNED is an in-depth look into how Ira Neimark became the successful CEO we all know him as today. From his start as a door boy at Bonwit Teller & Co. to his tenure as the CEO of Bergdorf Goodman, Ira put a lifetime of hard work into his illustrious career. This book is the fruit of that labor—a detailed account of everything he learned along the way and how he was able to position himself for success every step of the way.

    I first met Ira at the Top Ten Asian American Business Awards, when he was a Keynote speaker for the event. I immediately became a fan of his and introduced myself to him the first chance I got. Since then, we've developed a friendship, and I've personally positioned him as a mentor of mine.

    This book supplements his first two works, *Fifth Avenue to Bergdorf Goodman* and *The Rise of Fashion and Lessons Learned at Bergdorf Goodman*, both of which I thoroughly enjoyed. Reading this book will give you the benefit of the invaluable lessons Ira learned at every stage of his career, and these lessons are applicable to all industries—not just the fashion industry. His commitment and approach to customer service is something all companies should apply to their business model. I plan to apply these lessons to my personal and professional life to better prepare myself for inevitable obstacles along the way.

This book is a must read, and I suggest keeping a copy nearby at all times. I have even required my leadership team to read all of Ira's books.

Russell Sarder
Author of *Learning* and *Effective Learning Methods*
Chairman & CEO of NetCom Learning

Table of Contents

Introduction 1

Career 3
    First Steps 5
    My Role Model 6
    Office Boy 7
    Wisdom from an Unexpected Source 9
    G. Fox & Co. 10
    An Unlikely Fairy Godfather 11
    Next Steps 13
    Transitions 15
    Harmonious Relations 16
    A Bad Strategy 17
    Ownership Changes 19
    Ethics 21
    Adapting 22

Leadership 25
    Gaining Acceptance 27
    Making Changes 28
    Tough Choices 29
    Management Styles 31
    Natural Disasters 32
    Good People 33
    Deal with Professionals 35
    Travel 36
    The Greatest Opportunity 37
    Leadership Talents 39
    Management by Walking Around 40

Crafting Success 41
Changing Direction 43
Uniqueness 45
A Critical Lesson 46
High Standards 47
Be Prepared 48
Competitors 49
Taking Advice 50
Europe 51
Royalty 52
No Amateurs 53
Setting a Standard 54
Never Talk to Angels 55
Outstanding People 56
The Competition 57

Networking 59
Back to Basics 61
Good Presentation 62
The Critical Question 63
Appearance 64

Merchandising 65
Who Is Most Important? 67
Merchandising Procedures 69
Spark Plugs and the Steering Wheel 71
The Magic Price 72
A Lower Price Store 73
Weeks of Supply 74
Children's Dresses 75
BFA's Rules 76
Old, Bold Merchants 77

The Top of the List 79
Repositioning 80
Three Ingredients 81
Italian Designers 82
The Missing Element 83
The Value of Gold 85
Positive Thinking 86
Showmanship 87
Fashion Soldiers 90
Profitability 91
No Magic Formula 93
Competition 94
Stealing Their Business 96
The Best Teachers 98
Fashion Shows 99
Observe Talent 100
Excellence 102
Customers Are Smart 103
The Men's Store 106

Public Relations 109
CEO of Bergdorf Goodman 111
The Press 112
Credibility 113

Introduction

THIS IS A MANUAL or a handbook, if you will. You might also consider it a guide or a "how-to" book. Whichever description you decide is the most satisfactory, it builds on my two business memoirs, *Crossing Fifth Avenue to Bergdorf Goodman* and *The Rise of Fashion and Lessons Learned at Bergdorf Goodman*.

The lessons it contains were compiled from both books and start way back—with the very first lesson I learned as a door boy at Bonwit Teller & Co., a long-ago Fifth Avenue luxury retailer. I quickly realized that opening doors for well-to-do customers would give me the opportunity to open the door to a business career for myself.

So I got my foot in the door, so to speak, as a door boy and then, by taking advantage of every opportunity available to me, launched myself from what began as a part-time Christmas job to a lifelong career in retailing.

The lessons in this book are divided into different sections:
- Career
- Leadership
- Merchandising
- Networking
- Public Relations

Each set of lessons is preceded by a brief anecdote that describes a specific experience in my six-decade retail career. Some lessons are so important that they are repeated in more than one section for emphasis.

One of my early heroes was Benjamin Franklin. It is my hope that this book, like his *Poor Richard's Almanac*, will provide words of wisdom to benefit those that have the patience to read what I have written.

Ira Neimark

Career

First Steps

THESE WERE THE FIRST lessons I learned—when I entered the business world at Christmas time in 1938.

Fortunately, I fit the bellhop-style uniform the pageboy at Bonwit Teller's 721 Club wore, so they hired me for a part-time Christmas job. After Christmas, I was kept on and promoted to assistant doorman. I quickly found that learning to greet customers by name helped get me recognized by management.

Lessons Learned

~ *To get the job, make sure you fit the uniform—or whatever else is required to get your foot in the door.*

~ *Whenever the situation requires innovation, innovate.*

~ *People like to be greeted by name and with eye contact. Simply doing this can bring you many advantages.*

~ *If you want your abilities to shine, make sure that the environment and the atmosphere of the company suit your personality.*

My Role Model

I SELECTED WILLIAM HOLMES, the president of Bonwit Teller & Co., as my role model. When he arrived in a chauffeured-driven limousine each morning, imposing and very well dressed, he was greeted with respect by everyone. He was inspirational and remained my role model throughout my business career.

My next promotion, from door boy to Bill Holmes' office boy, meant that I no longer received customer tips—my other income. But it was more than worth the loss.

Lessons Learned

~ *Selecting an ideal role model at an early age is important and requires mature judgment. Those who select well go on to success. Those who do not will have a much more difficult row to hoe.*

~ *It is sometimes wise to accept a reduction in salary or position, if it leads to greater opportunity.*

~ *Always bet with other people's money.*

Office Boy

SERVING AS OFFICE BOY to the president of Bonwit Teller & Co. and observing how he operated—with visiting retail leaders and fashion executives, as well as employees and customers throughout the store—set an example for me that I never forgot.

Everyone in the store admired him.

Lessons Learned

~ *It is not so much what you know, but how you execute what you know.*

~ *Opportunity is always all around you. Another key to success is the ability to identify and develop the opportunity.*

~ *When you plan your career, aim as high as you can. You may not hit the target at the top, but you'll come much closer than you will if you don't aim high.*

~ *Never forget salespeople, designers, and manufacturers. If you have them on your side, you will be a successful merchant.*

~ *Putting yourself in the mind of the customer, and learning what she thinks her requirement is, is half the battle. The other half is meeting that requirement.*

~ *If you are going to be a merchant you have to gamble on your judgment. If your judgment is poor, you will be poor.*

Wisdom from an Unexpected Source

DURING WORLD WAR II, while I was stationed in Hawaii, I received a Christmas check from Bonwit Teller & Co. I cashed it at a bar called Pi Wy Chong. I later realized that if my employer knew that I was drinking on their money, my reputation might be tarnished. It wasn't.

Lessons Learned

~ *Drink if you will, but not on other people's money.*

~ *If you want to create a good impression, always let your management know that you are interested in and dedicated to your job.*

G. Fox & Co.

I WAS ALWAYS LOOKING for a more professional and successful method of managing inventories. I found the solution by examining the many procedures used by New England retailers.

The successful procedure led to my being invited by Beatrice Fox Auerbach to join G. Fox & Co. in Hartford, Connecticut. I eventually became the executive vice president, general merchandising manager of that famous store. This was where I learned to run a store.

Lessons Learned

~ *If you don't know how to make a merchandising procedure successful, keep your eyes and ears open until you find the person who has the answer.*

~ *It is most important to know the background and history of the company in which you hope to build your career. This not only helps you understand and appreciate the culture and background of the successful executives you will be working with, it allows you to "fit into" that culture.*

~ *The starting salary for a new job should be of secondary importance. It is the opportunity the job offers for the future that is important.*

An Unlikely Fairy Godfather

I JOINED G. FOX & CO., one of the outstanding retailers in the country, to build my career. However, two years later, Beatrice Fox Auerbach asked me to be the president of Brown Thompson, her retail stepchild.

I was prepared to refuse the offer when my mentor, Bill Holmes, who was also my rabbi, advised me to accept it. He gave me one good reason.

"BFA offered you the job because she needs help," he said. "If you refuse she will always remember that when she needed you, you turned her down." His advice assured my future with BFA.

Lessons Learned

~ *If you possibly can, find a fairy godmother, or godfather (sometimes called a rabbi), to guide you through the minefields of the business world. He or she can keep you pointed in the right direction to reach your goals.*

~ *Again, it is what you know and who you know that get results. It never hurts, and is usually very helpful, to know people in high places.*

~ *When you adjust to a new position, examine carefully your predecessor's successes and failures before you embark on a different strategy.*

~ *The more you can think and shop like your customer, not like a buyer, the more successful you will be.*

Next Steps

AT G. FOX AND CO., I got to know the top executives of some of the leading retailers in the country. I was especially fortunate to meet the senior executives of B. Altman & Co. I admired the company and hoped to be invited to become their executive vice president, general merchandise manager.
It was one of the finest stores in America.

Lessons Learned

~ *Deciding when to leave one position for another requires careful consideration of your career objectives. Additional advice from experienced executives should be part of the final decision.*

~ *Whenever possible, associate with successful business executives. Smart executives are always looking for talented people. It is better to be known than to be a face in the crowd.*

~ *Whenever you are offered a job opportunity, it is most desirable, if possible, to clear the decision with the former as well as the future employer. This will not be possible in all cases, but the effort should be made, if for no other reason than the executives will likely see each other over the years at social and business events.*

~ *A new position offers new opportunities. It is important to integrate slowly into the company so that people come to feel they know you and what you stand for. Acceptance cannot be achieved overnight. As difficult as it may be, patience will always win out.*

Transitions

MY EXPERIENCE AT BOTH G. Fox & Co. and B. Altman & Co. taught me how to overcome the politics of being the outsider brought in over present senior executives. Developing close relationships with my competition eased the transition.

Lessons Learned

~ *Whenever a new executive joins a company, the other executives will circle like sharks attempting to find his or her weak spots. Tact and superior knowledge will win out.*

~ *If for any reason you are going to take the risk of contradicting your boss, be sure that whatever it is you do will be a success.*

Harmonious Relations

WHEN G. FOX & CO. MADE the decision to expand its store in Hartford by thousands of feet, all the senior executives were asked for their recommendations. All the submitted opinions had merit, but making use of my experience with branch stores, both at Bonwit Teller & Co. and Gladding's, I presented a well-organized, detailed analysis of the proper use of the new space that would become available.

In addition to presenting the plan to the CEO, I sent copies to all the senior executives. This eliminated any animosity within the organization.

Lessons Learned

~ *When one of the highest executives in the company asks you for ideas or suggestions, it is important to keep the key executives in the loop. They will not like being upstaged, but will appreciate that they were not kept in the dark. This also gives them the ability to comment negatively or positively on your presentation, instead of just sitting there with egg on their faces.*

A Bad Strategy

TO PREPARE FOR JOINING G. Fox & Co., I developed an analysis comparing G. Fox & Co. advertising, by classification, to Bloomingdale's and B. Altman's in New York. The analysis showed that, in some classifications, G. Fox & Co. advertised merchandise prices that were much lower than both of those stores. The reason for this is that the man I was to report to accepted all the vendor-paid advertising on lower price merchandise instead of advertising what G. Fox stood for.

Upstaging the boss is a bad strategy for advancement.

Lessons Learned

~ *Never present the person that you are hoping to replace with an analysis showing how wrong his strategy is when compared to other leaders in the business.*

~ *No matter how undesirable a request from management may be, consider the long–range implications. As in many situations in life, you must calculate if the gamble is worth taking. Seeking good advice from people with successful experience will help you to arrive at the correct decision.*

~ *It is important to become familiar with the background and culture of the company you join. The owners and principals will require that executives demonstrate they understand the company's business principles and will appreciate that they show interest in the company as a matter of pride.*

~ *If management wants you to take on an unpleasant assignment, as difficult a decision as it may be, do it understanding that the risk may exceed the reward in the long run.*

Ownership Changes

THROUGHOUT MY CAREER, from Bonwit Teller & Co. to Bergdorf Goodman, some of the retailers that I worked for changed ownership for one reason or another. This is always a traumatic experience for everyone. The following lessons will give you an idea of what to expect and how to react successfully.

Lessons Learned

- *Whenever there is a change in ownership in any business, the new owner will invariably have management changes. Executives at different ages have different challenges in mind.*
  - *The young executive is usually protected by lack of seniority and can ride out, and may benefit from, the change.*
  - *The senior executive is usually most at risk. Be prepared for a change in your position—either for someone to replace you, or for an executive above you who will want the change.*
  - *In the case of the senior executive, keep your options open by always being discretely aware of the opportunities that are available to you in other companies.*

~ Keep your nose to the grindstone. Working hard and long to achieve your objectives is bound to be recognized—by your superiors and your colleagues, as well as your competition.

~ Try not to show your frustration when management changes that you have no control over take place. Do your job to the best of your ability, and keep your eyes open for opportunities at another company that will appreciate your talents

Ethics

FROM THE VERY BEGINNING, I carefully studied the successful chief executives that I had the opportunity to work for. Each one, from Bill Holmes at Bonwit Teller & Co. to Beatrice Fox Auerbach at G. Fox & Co., had many important lessons to teach me. Ethics and reputation were at the top of all of their lists

Lessons Learned

~ *Business principles and standards must be set and maintained. You must never compromise your principles—what you stand for—and never lower your standards.*

~ *Retailers, and all business people for that matter, should make ethics their first consideration when they evaluate any opportunity. Fine reputations can be destroyed by lapses in good and honest judgment.*

~ *To be a good businessman you must also be a good citizen. As high standards are required in a successful business, so they are required in the society that surrounds us. Catering to the lowest denominator will eventually bring you there*

Adapting

MEETING AND LEARNING FROM experienced professionals in all types of careers will help you adapt to different social and business situations as they arise. I learned this early on and it held true throughout my career.

Lessons Learned

~ *The saying, "When in Rome, do as the Romans do," applies to all countries and unusual environments.*

~ *Whenever you find yourself in an unfamiliar situation, let an experienced person advise you.*

~ *Whenever an opportunity presents itself, even though it may not be in the short- or long-range plan, examine the opportunity very carefully from every angle. Use all your best thinking, as well as the counsel of those who work with you. As President Woodrow Wilson remarked on the subject of decision-making, "I not only use all the brains I have, but all that I can borrow."*

~ *Opportunity is always there if you continue to look for it. The phrase, "It is not what you know, but who you know" is only half correct. I believe, "It is what you know and who you know," that brings success to your dreams and ambitions.*

~ *No matter what the business, basic principles that successful executives have proven to be sound will, more times than not, lead to success.*

Leadership

Gaining Acceptance

IT WAS MY GOOD FORTUNE that Beatrice Fox Auerbach, the owner of G. Fox & Co., heard my presentation on inventory management at the Frederic Atkins Store Principles Meeting. BFA was one of the very few store principals who appreciated the importance of inventory management.

When she hired me in an executive position at G. Fox & Co., I had to earn the respect of the other executives in order to be accepted.

Lessons Learned

~ *It is not so much what you know, but how you execute what you know.*

~ *When you adjust to a new position, examine carefully your predecessor's successes and failures before you embark on a different strategy.*

Making Changes

MANY EXECTIVES DID NOT understand, or want to understand, my method of inventory management. Many failed on their own. Others were asked to work elsewhere.

Lessons Learned

~ *Convincing people to use an unfamiliar method is always a difficult task. Motivating them to change requires convincing them that the change will benefit them greatly. If they can't be motivated, they must be directed. If they can't be directed, they should be removed.*

~ *Whenever you are offered a job opportunity, it is most desirable, if possible, to clear the decision with the former as well as the future employer. This will not be possible in all cases, but the effort should be made, if for no other reason than the executives will likely see each other over the years at social and business events.*

~ *If you are put in the position of competing with your peers publicly, develop a business strategy that allows you to make a good showing.*

Tough Choices

AFTER LEAVING A WONDERFUL position at Gladding's in Providence, Rhode Island to join G. Fox & Co. in Hartford, Connecticut as assistant general merchandising manager, I was asked by BFA to leave G. Fox & Co. to become president of Brown Thompson, her very substandard department store. The title may have been great, but it was an inferior store with no future

I learned the following, very tough lessons from the experience.

Lessons Learned

~ *No matter how undesirable a request from management may be, consider the long–range implications. As in many situations in life, you must calculate if the gamble is worth taking. Seeking good advice from people with successful experience will help you to arrive at the correct decision.*

~ *It is important to become familiar with the background and culture of the company you join. The owners and principals will require that executives demonstrate they understand the company's business principles and will appreciate that they show interest in the company as a matter of pride.*

~ *If management wants you to take on an unpleasant assignment, as difficult a decision as it may be, do it understanding that the risk may exceed the reward in the long run*

~ *No matter what type of business you are involved in, decide who you want to be and what customer you want to appeal to.*

~ *When the past is bleak and the present is not much better, motivating an organization requires enthusiasm and courage. Make sure everyone in the organization understands the plan is in broad detail. Outline the plan in greater detail to the organization's managers. And be "consistently consistent."*

~ *Articulate what your standards are, and to be sure that those standards are monitored frequently and consistently. It is critical that all of the organization's employees understand what is required of them.*

Management Styles

BEATRICE FOX AURBACH BELIEVED in customer service above all else. Her customer service philosophy was drilled into each and every employee. Unfortunately, when G. Fox & Co. was sold to The May Department Stores Company, all that was lost.

The difference in management styles left me with an impression that I never forgot.

Lessons Learned

> ~ *Whenever a question arises, regarding customer service for example, no one should have to go to the company manual for an answer. Employees should be able to ask themselves, "What would management expect me to do in this situation?" And act accordingly. This approach will work many more times than not.*

Natural Disasters

WHEN THE MAY DEPARTMENT STORES COMPANY merged with (bought) G. Fox & Co., the whole customer service concept that BFA inculcated was changed. Even my position as general merchandising manager was challenged.

The May Department Stores Company wanted to replace me with their man. BFA said no. She felt that I knew how she wanted the store to be run. The May Company had a different retail philosophy.

Lessons Learned

~ *Nothing is forever, good times or bad. Be aware of this and always be prepared for the possibility of an ownership change—as you would be for any natural disaster.*

Good People

EVEN IN DIFFICULT TRANSTITIONS there are talented people who stand out. I recruited Dawn Mello from The May Department Stores Company, first to fashion director at B. Altman & Co. and then to the same position at Bergdorf Goodman.

Lessons Learned

~ *In all difficult situations, there are things to learn and good people to meet.*

~ *No matter how professional and successful a company might be, particularly in a takeover, if the new business culture is different enough to make you feel ineffective and untrue to your potential, consider how to move on. Otherwise, in the long run, there will be unhappiness and frustration on both sides—a double negative not worth enduring.*

~ *Whenever there is a change in ownership in any business, the new owner will invariably have management changes. Executives at different ages have different challenges in mind.*

- *The young executive is usually protected by lack of seniority and can ride out, and may benefit from, the change.*
- *The senior executive is usually most at risk. Be prepared for a change in your position—either for someone to replace you, or for an executive above you who will want the change.*
- *In the case of the senior executive, keep your options open by always being discretely aware of the opportunities that are available to you in other companies.*

Deal with Professionals

BEFORE I LEFT G. FOX & Co. for B. Altman & Co., I had the opportunity to recruit Robert Suslow from Bloomingdale's to become assistant general merchandise manager. Bob eventually left the May Department Stores Company to become one of the top executives at Saks Fifth Avenue.

I fortunately recognized, though not in all cases, ambitious people with talent.

Lessons Learned

~ *Always look for smart people. The way to tell if they are smart is to see how sincere they are in describing their personal ambitions. If their ambitions are similar to yours, you will be able to tell how sincere they are by understanding and relating to their goals and objectives.*

~ *If you can help it, never deal with amateurs, or people who don't know how to maximize their responsibilities. Find a professional—it makes life easier and more profitable for everyone.*

~ *In every business it is important to know the major players well. Being able to talk with them and learn from their experiences will always broaden your knowledge.*

Travel

MY NEXT PIECE OF GOOD FORTUNE and networking led me to become the general merchandising manager at B. Altman & Co. in New York. One of my first assignments was to meet all B. Altman's commissionaires around the world. That trip lasted six long weeks.

But it was an experience like no other, and it gave me the opportunity for an education I could acquire nowhere else. I took full advantage of it.

Lessons Learned

~ *Travel will always broaden your experiences. Explore every opportunity. The best opportunities may come from the most unexpected places.*

~ *Remember the possibility that a single, well-executed transaction, each year, can cover your annual salary. If you find it, you will be rewarded and appreciated by everyone involved in your future.*

~ *Seek out smart women in the business world and learn what they think. They can really help you understand your woman customer.*

~ *Whenever you get the opportunity to meet the leaders of your industry, do so.*

The Greatest Opportunity

MY PERFORMANCE AT G. FOX & CO. and B. Altman & Co. brought me to the attention of Carter Hawley Hale, who had recently purchased Bergdorf Goodman. I was hired from B. Altman & Co. to be president and CEO of this exceptional fashion store. This was to be the greatest opportunity of all.

Lessons Learned

~ *As uplifting a feeling as it is to join a company that you have long admired—as the CEO or in any other major management position—it is very important that both you and the previous management of that company have a specific and clearly written understanding of the job responsibilities of all the executives involved.*

~ *As difficult as it is to leave a company that you feel has been helpful in your career, and particularly if you are close to the senior executives, it is very important to leave on the best of terms possible. Your paths will undoubtedly cross many times.*

~ *Whenever you take on a new responsibility, it is imperative to study the previous administration's strategies, as well as its strengths and weaknesses. Apply the same study to your competition.*

~ *Business executives who are insulated and live in a vacuum tend not to see growth opportunities. It is important to measure your performance against your peers'. One of the first measurements is productivity, that is, sales per square foot. The second is gross profit per square foot. These comparisons are easily available if you look for them. The next important step is to act on the information.*

Leadership Talents

LEADERSHIP REQUIRES MANY different talents. I applied the following leadership lessons to raise the fashion image and financial performance of Bergdorf Goodman.

Lessons Learned

~ *Business principles and standards must be set and maintained. You must never compromise your principles—what you stand for— and never lower your standards.*

~ *When you are taking over an underperforming business, it is important to analyze the strengths as well as the weaknesses of the business. The strengths should be developed and the weaknesses eliminated. This applies to merchandise as well as people.*

~ *All levels of personnel in any business must know the company's goals and ambitions. When they carry out their responsibilities, they must reflect the chief executive's vision.*

~ *Retailers, and all business people for that matter, should make ethics their first consideration when they evaluate any opportunity. Fine reputations can be destroyed by lapses in good and honest judgement.*

Management by Walking Around

WHEN I WALKED THROUGH THE STORES that I worked for, I always talked to the salespeople about what their customers wanted. I found this approach invaluable to understanding my present customers, as well as discovering what it took to attract customers away from my competition.

I referred to this as getting my MBWA degree—Management by Walking Around. The approach turned into a winning strategy for me, one ignored by many retailers today.

Lessons Learned

~ *Asking customers, as well as professionals, their opinions of your efforts will give you some candid thoughts you may not have been aware of.*

~ *To build a business you have to know both who your present customer is, and who you want your new customer to be. After that, the objective is to decide what type of operation or service will satisfy them both.*

Crafting Success

ATTRACTING THE HIGHEST profile fashion designers in Paris, Milan, and New York helped us revive Bergdorf Goodman's fashion reputation. And it brought us sales to match that reputation.

This was done over fierce objections from our competition.

Lessons Learned

~ *When you're trying to revitalize a business, there is almost always something—a trend, product line, or expert—that has enough industry recognition to redefine your company's meaning for customers. As soon as you discover this critical element, it is imperative that you pull out all the stops to align your company with this new direction.*

~ *Three things are required to create a successful business—fashion or otherwise:*
  1. *Is the concept correct for the business? As a corollary, what does the business stand for?*
  2. *Is the financing appropriate?*
  3. *Is the organization professional?*

  All three are required. Otherwise, the business will collapse like a house of cards.

~ *Successful business relationships are best developed when both parties understand and agree on their mutual objectives. Writing down these objectives will help eliminate any misunderstanding.*

~ *If you believe what you are doing is right, stick to your guns. Successful results will overcome nearly all adversity.*

~ *Whenever you take on a responsibility that requires the involvement of the previous executive, make sure you both go in with a clear understanding of each party's responsibilities. Understood that, in most cases, the previous executive will be reluctant to turn over responsibilities in areas in which he feels he has a superior background*

~ *It is important to be successful in your initial changes in order to convince everyone involved that you are on the right track. The more people who tell management that they made the right decision to bring you on board, the easier the transition will be.*

Changing Direction

CHANGING BERGDORF GOODMAN'S DIRECTION required constant communication, good and bad, with all the people involved. A number of executives could not or would not understand the changes required to accomplish our long-term objectives. Unfortunately they had to be removed for the up-and-coming fashion talent.

Lessons Learned

~ *Constant communication with your market principals and your own executives minimizes the possibility of signal or direction confusion.*

~ *When the Chairman asks you to lunch, and you have a previous appointment for an important lunch, invite the Chairman along.*

~ *Financial executives tend to view a business from the expense reduction viewpoint. Merchants view a business in terms of its growth opportunities. Both are right. However, it becomes a matter of not putting the cart before the horse. A merchant's responsibility is to build sales profitably.*

Financial people should manage expenses in order to grow the profit of the business. But without sales growth, there will be no additional expenses to manage.

~ *When a company makes a strategic decision, it is critical that all concerned—executives employees, suppliers, customers, and the press—be given the positive reasons for the decision. Otherwise negative thinking can snowball. Sometimes selling the positive is like pushing water uphill. But the positive must prevail.*

Uniqueness

STORES AS DIFFERENT AS Bergdorf Goodman and Apple Inc. have created a "customer buying experience," and built loyal customers and a very profitable business. The retailers that do this well will prosper. Those that don't will disappear.

Lessons Learned

~ *"Build a better mousetrap" and "build a great baseball team and they will come," are not empty phrases. If a business's management stresses service and uniqueness, and maintains a complete and broad assortment of whatever is to be sold, the business will be a success.*

~ *Short-range planning will help to keep you in business a short time. Long-range planning will keep you there much longer.*

~ *When you only have a little control over a situation, a lot of luck helps.*

~ *When the business isn't doing well, and has weak management, consultants are helpful, but there is no substitute for professional management—professional management being defined as "proven professionals."*

A Critical Lesson

IF YOU ARE BUILDING AN organization or giving advice to associates, the following lesson is important to master.

Lessons Learned

~ *When you are searching for a key executive for your organization, make sure you define the position clearly and that everyone involved understands the standards and goals set for the position. In addition, employ every resource—from personal contacts to a professional executive recruiter familiar with all aspects of your industry's inner workings—to locate the best candidate. Unimpeachable references are an imperative requirement.*

High Standards

ALWAYS LOOKING FOR A NEW IDEA is as imperative to success as beating the competition. And maintaining high standards will always work. Standards should always be set at the highest level. By observing some competitors, I found that when top management neglects high standards their employees do as well.

Lessons Learned

~ *Never be satisfied with your progress. There is always another idea, different from your competitor's. Competition is a threat to your business success. Study your competitors carefully, and fight them aggressively.*

~ *To be a good businessman you must also be a good citizen. As high standards are required in a successful business, so they are required in the society that surrounds us. Catering to the lowest common denominator will eventually bring you there.*

Be Prepared

WHENEVER I PREPARED for business meetings, employment opportunities, or whatever, I found that my old Boy Scout motto, "Always be prepared" worked well. It still does.

Lessons Learned

~ *In today's business world, all types of tests are required to determine the qualifications for a job applicant—from clericals to the CEO. It is best to learn as much as possible about the type of questions that will be asked and the testing that will be done. There are books and manuals about any subject under the sun. The wise approach: never go unprepared.*

~ *One of the defining moments of a career is the first impression you make on the executives who will be instrumental in guiding you and deciding your future in the business world.*

Competitors

I STUDIED MY COMPETITORS very carefully, learned from them, and copied from them when necessary.

Lessons Learned

~ *When you revive or develop a business, it is imperative to have the wholehearted support of those who appointed you to that responsibility. Proper business principles, patience, and fortitude applied to the project will reward you with success.*

~ *Successful competitors have usually figured out the necessary steps to becoming industry leaders. This was true for Henri Bendel, across the street from Bergdorf Goodman, as well as for Bloomingdale's a few blocks away.*

The expression "steal their business" may not sound "professional" or much like a marketing strategy, but it is what Bergdorf Goodman had to do to become a dominant force in the fashion industry.

~ *The first step in growing a business to its potential is a sound and imaginative marketing strategy. No matter how large or small, a company must have a professional and talented organization, and specific direction from the company's objectives.*

Taking Advice

THERE ARE ALL KINDS OF advice out there.

A lesson I learned at Bergdorf Goodman is to ask more than one company for their opinions about your future marketing plans.

Lessons Learned

~ *Accounting firms and financial advisors, in some cases, over-emphasize retail opportunities—as when they recommended Bergdorf Goodman open a branch store in Chicago. In other cases, they underestimate retail opportunities—such as Barneys New York's great potential.*

Europe

I TRAVELED TO EUROPE TO attract talented fashion designers to Bergdorf Goodman. Attracting Fendi from Rome and Yves Saint Laurent from Paris was a turning point. Each led me on an adventure never to be forgotten

Lessons Learned

- *Everyone wants to visit the great cities of the world. With hard work, patience, and fortitude, you can achieve this dream. Make your visits even more worthwhile by finding and engaging international talent.*

- *When a business has lost its position of leadership in any industry, it is imperative for that business to change direction in order to capture the attention of lost customers, as well as to attract a new audience.*

Royalty

I LEARNED BUSINESS ethics early in my career. I also learned how to handle myself and dress properly when meeting royalty, or other high-profile people, at special events.

A person who dresses properly for special occasions attracts attention from people who can help his or her career. Those who don't, don't.

Lessons Learned

~ *There is a time for business and a time for fun. Treat each accordingly. Business relationships are just that. It is best to never to accept a gift that cannot be consumed or eaten at one sitting. This is still good advice.*

~ *When you get the opportunity to meet royalty, or other high-profile celebrities and business executives, it is important to wear the proper clothes and open with an appropriate greeting so that you make a lasting favorable impression.*

No Amateurs

HAVING THE PROPER TEAM of proven professionals on board is another imperative. This is no place for amateurs.

Lessons Learned

~ *Whatever the task, everyone involved should enthusiastically understand, accept, and support the company's vision and direction. Employees unwilling or unable to understand the vision should be released to work for the competition.*

Setting a Standard

PRIVATE CITIZENS RESTORED the magnificent Pulitzer Pomona Fountain at The Grand Army Plaza on Fifth Avenue. Leaving this magnificent fountain to stand in neglect was not an option.

Lessons Learned

~ *When a city's administration has too many different priorities and constituents to satisfy, many beautiful areas can be neglected. As in this example, private (business) donors can set a standard for others to follow.*

Never Talk to Angels

MANY YEARS AGO, Bonwit Teller's head personal shopper left her valuable customers book in a taxicab and panic reigned.

However, Bill Holmes, the president of Bonwit Teller & Co., called Jim Farley, the postmaster general. Jim Farley called Mayor Fiorello LaGuardia. The customer book was found and returned in a matter of hours.

This was a lesson I learned at an early age and used effectively whenever needed.

Lessons Learned

~ *If you want a project to come to a successful conclusion, go to the head of the organization involved.*

The expression, "Never talk to angels when you can talk to God," always made sense to me and brought me many more successes than failures

~ *As everyone knows today: Never make a presentation to the executives who are in a position to decide your business future without first having a dry run so that you are sure everything is in order.*

Outstanding People

MEETING OUTSANDING PEOPLE, like Estée Lauder, Princess Diana, Andy Warhol, and many others, helped inspire me to reach my highest goals. I found that I could always learn something by observing these high-profile people.

Lessons Learned

~ *Whenever you meet an outstanding personality, in business, art, or whatever, always try to obtain a memento of the meeting for future reference and networking. At the very least, a business card will do.*

~ *In every company, large and small, you will have the opportunity to form business relationships with other companies led by outstanding executives with inspirational qualities.*

It is important to identify these people. Slowly, but surely, let them become aware of your interest in their accomplishments and of your own ambitions.

The Competition

MY BUSINESS PLANS WERE always initiated by my awareness of my competitors' strategy. All my executives had to be aware of the competition as well. Ignore the competition at your own peril.

Lessons Learned

~ *When you develop a business plan, it is critical to know all the players and how each, in turn, will fit into making your strategy and business model a success. As in chess or checkers, be aware of each player's goals and be sure their moves benefit your objectives, not theirs.*

~ *This is so important that it bears repeating: When you recruit top management executives, it is imperative to research all the people and all the performance records available, to be sure the final decision will benefit you and your business. It is better to make no move at all than to select the wrong person.*

~ *Take the opportunity to visit every business that relates to your own. The networking of meeting one executive and then being introduced to the next is like compound interest—your business relationships will grow and grow.*

~ *I repeat: It is what you know and who you know that gets results. It never hurts and is very helpful to know people in high places. Whenever possible, associate with successful business executives. Smart executives are always looking for talented people. It is better to be known than to be a face in the crowd.*

Networking

Benjamin Franklin said it two hundred years ago: "Every turning point in the great man's life story required some deft combination of hard work and personal connections."

Back to Basics

I QUICKLY LEARNED THAT those retailers whose businesses fail do not pay attention to a very basic retail principle. Know what is happening on the selling floor—whether it be in one store or in hundreds.

Again, manage by walking around (MBWA). It is and always was great exercise.

Lessons Learned

~ *Nearly every retailer, many still in business and some recently departed, has at some point realized, sometimes, finally, when it was too late, that it has over-expanded. In the process, some of those retailers over-inventoried to the point of financial disaster—in some cases worse than that of The Great Depression.*

Many retailers, eager to reduce their expenses, make the cataclysmic error of drastically reducing their salespeople so that customers are left to look in vain for a sales person to make a sale. Example: Circuit City.

Good Presentation

GOOD PRESENTATION, I LEARNED, helped determine how people viewed me, my store, and my people—as well as my customers. Advertising will help, but good public relations are better.

Lessons Learned

~ *If you want to reach your audience in the most positive terms, it is important to ensure that you are publicly associated and featured with the leaders of your field of endeavor. Good public relations will move a business on to success. Bad or negative public relations will help lead to its demise.*

The Critical Question

WHO ARE MY CUSTOMERS? I learned to ask that question very early in the game.

It merits repeating: I found that by walking around, store after store, talking to sales people and customers, I benefitted greatly both in knowledge and exercise.

Lessons Learned

> ~ *In any business, it is imperative to know as much as possible about your present and potential customer. Focus groups, like political pollsters, must ask the right people the right questions in order to get the right answers. Otherwise, they generate the wrong answers and simply add to the confusion. The focus group should be your own customers. They, more than anyone, know what they like about your business and what it is they don't like.*

Appearance

FROM THE VERY BEGINNING, each and every one of my mentors taught me the importance of high standards—both in my appearance, as well as in my business surroundings.

Lessons Learned

~ *Dressing is like packaging. An attractive package is always front and center. The unattractive package is usually moved to the rear of the shelf.*

~ *To be a good businessman you must also be a good citizen. As high standards are required in a successful business, so they are required in the society that surrounds us. Catering to the lowest common denominator will eventually bring you there.*

MERCHANDISING

Who Is Most Important?

AS OFFICE BOY TO the president of Bonwit Teller & Co., I observed closely and learned that the company held designers, manufactures, sales people, and, most of all, customers in very high regard.

As a lowly stock boy in the handbag department, I learned that salespeople were key to satisfying the customers' requests, as well as making the sale.

Lessons Learned

~ *Never forget, sales people, designers, and manufacturers. If you have them on your side, you will be a successful merchant.*

~ *Putting yourself in the mind of the customer, and learning what they think is their requirement is, is half the battle. The other half is meeting that requirement.*

~ *If you are going to be a merchant you have to gamble on your judgment. If your judgment is poor, you will be poor.*

~ *Salespeople always know what merchandise is easiest to sell. They can spot a bestseller before the buyers can. They can in, most cases, tell what isn't going to be easy to sell, and they can also tell at what price it should and will sell for.*

~ *Repeat: If you have the salespeople on your side you will succeed. If the salespeople are not, you will increase your chances of failure.*

Merchandising Procedures

EARLY ON, WHEN I RETURNED from the war in 1946 and was appointed assistant merchandising manager at Bonwit Teller & Co., I realized that developing merchandise budgets for buyers was a flawed procedure, causing unbalanced inventories and unnecessary markdowns. The challenge to improve that took years to figure out. But the rewards far outweighed the time I spent to find the solution.

Lessons Learned

~ *If you don't know how or why to make a merchandising procedure successful, keep your eyes and ears open until you find the person who has the answer.*

~ *The major reason for high markdowns and lower profit in many retail enterprises is the lack of professional planning practices.*

~ *In many cases, when a successful retailer—defined as a strong sales and profit growth company, with a growing customer base—is purchased, the new owner is too hasty in changing the store to fit his concept. In more cases than not, this is the recipe for failure.*

~ *Slow moving and old inventory will strangle any business; no matter how many management changes are made.*

~ *A ready-to-wear inventory is only as good as its newest merchandise.*

Spark Plugs and the Steering Wheel

I OFTEN COMPARE salespeople to the spark plugs in a car. To continue the simile, buyers are the steering wheel. A professional buyer has the ability to steer the business in the right direction.

An amateur will steer his or her business to its demise.

Removing the spark plugs from a car to save gas is as stupid as removing salespeople from the selling floor to reduce expenses.

Lessons Learned

~ *Never, ever appoint a person to be a buyer unless he or she has been a proven success as an assistant buyer. A rare exception may be made if the buyer candidate is very bright, and has a smart merchandising manager to give direction and supervision.*

~ *In retailing there are many important positions, but none as important as a talented buyer. Executives who can identify, develop, and encourage talent are critical to a retailer's success.*

The Magic Price

RETAILERS, AT ALL LEVELS of the business, will decide on retail prices by using all the right variables. But I learned early on that the place to start is with the question, "What price will the customer pay?" This is particularly true of sale merchandise.

Lessons Learned

~ *There is always a magic price. The trick, if you will, is to be realistic and determine at what price customers will really be excited. Too many times buyers will decide on a price they believe or hope will make the sale a success, not that the customer will find exciting.*

~ *The buyer's ability to correctly find and negotiate the "magic price" has always been the most successful formula for moving sale merchandise. Filene's Basement understood this better than many regular retailers ever did.*

A Lower Price Store

WHEN I MOVED TO a lower price store, I made the initial error of not taking into account the lower price customer. It didn't take me long to correct my mistake.

Lessons Learned

~ *When you adjust to a new position, examine carefully your predecessor's successes and failures before you embark on a different strategy.*

~ *The more you can think and shop like your customer, not like a buyer, the more successful you will be.*

~ *A good merchant should have an organized sense of urgency. Not taking the immediate steps necessary to move slow moving, unwanted merchandise, to make room for new, desirable merchandise, has led to the demise of more retailers than I dare to count.*

Weeks of Supply

MY SEARCH TO FIND and to develop a sound merchandising procedure to plan inventories properly came to a successful conclusion when I discovered the "Units Weeks of Supply" calculation.

This, undoubtedly, was a merchandising concept that elevated me as a profitable merchant above many of my peers.

Lessons Learned

~ *Retailing does not exist in a vacuum. All the information you need to be a successful merchant is out there—if you have the sense to know what you should be looking for, and where to look for it.*

~ *Convincing people to use an unfamiliar method is always a difficult task. Motivating them to change requires convincing them that the change will benefit them greatly. If they can't be motivated, they must be directed. If they can't be directed, they should be removed.*

~ *Don't wait for desirable merchandise or opportunities to come to you. You must go after both.*

Children's Dresses

WHEN BEATRICE FOX AUERBACH criticized Stanley Marcus, of Neiman Marcus, for not having a proper assortment of children's dresses, I learned an important lesson. I had asked BFA, when we were in Dallas, to help me pick out a dress for Janie, my young daughter. The assortment of children's dresses was awful.

Lessons Learned

~ *When a retailer has made an investment and commitment to be in business, the customer has a right to expect that he will also fulfill his responsibility of carrying a complete assortment of whatever it is the store sells.*

~ *Watch every trend in retail distribution. There are new concepts being developed every day—some successful, some not. Analyze the successful trends to see if any part of them can be used to your advantage.*

~ *No matter what type of business you are involved in, decide who you want to be and what customer you want to appeal to.*

BFA's Rules

RETAILERS MUST MAINTAIN an in-stock assortment of basic merchandise at all times. I recall BFA, figuratively speaking, beating that rule into me every day of every week.

As important, when slow-selling merchandise is sitting around, "Mark it down and buy something that your customers want." Simple.

Lessons Learned

> ~ *In retail, as in many other types of businesses, maintaining basic stock books, now computer programmed, is a given. Just like brushing your teeth, do it at least twice a day. No imagination is required, but it has to be done. When you turn on the light switch, you expect the light to go on. When a customer asks for a basic item or size, he or she expects it to be in stock. The alternative is not only a lost sale, but also the potential loss of the customer.*

> ~ *The taking of markdowns can be developed into a profitable way to do business if the markdown is taken early enough, allowing money from the sale of the reduced merchandise to be reinvested in new merchandise. Experience shows that most buyers, and very few divisional merchandise managers, know or care to do this. Hence, lost business, lower gross margins, and, eventually, red ink on the bottom line.*

Old, Bold Merchants

I HAVE OFTEN FELT THAT, like pilots, there are old merchants and bold merchants, but not many old, bold merchants. Bold merchants take risks that can be very rewarding. The caveat is to be careful of what is up ahead. Too many stores and too much inventory can bring you down.

Lessons Learned

~ *Finding and identifying talented merchants is critical to success. Therefore, a potential candidate must demonstrate his or her merchandising ability. You can best determine this by observing how aware a merchant is of current trends. He or she should be not too attached to what was, but more interested in what will be.*

~ *Whenever a resource selects your store (no matter how large or small) for the introduction of a new product, the executive concerned must notify the senior executive so that the product is judged by more than one person.*

~ *Business executives who are insulated and live in a vacuum tend not to see growth opportunities. It is important to measure your performance against your peers'. One of the first measurements is productivity, that is, sales per square foot. The second is gross profit per square foot. These comparisons are easily available if you look for them. The next important step is to act on the information.*

~ *When you are taking over an underperforming business, it is important to analyze the strengths as well as the weaknesses of the business. The strengths should be developed and the weaknesses eliminated. This applies to merchandise as well as people.*

The Top of the List

THIS LESSON CAME WHEN, shortly after I joined Bergdorf Goodman, I was asked to become the president of Lord and Taylor. As fine a compliment and opportunity as it was, business ethics dictated my commitment to the principals at Bergdorf Goodman

Lessons Learned

~ *Retailers, and all business people for that matter, should make ethics their first consideration when they evaluate any opportunity. Fine reputations can be destroyed by lapses in good and honest judgment.*

Repositioning

WHEN YOU WANT TO REPOSITION a retail company, or any business, key executives who can help the CEO to understand and define the past, present and future customer will give you a far greater chance of success than experimentation will. A top-flight fashion office at Bergdorf Goodman gave us this direction.

Lessons Learned

~ *To imbue a store with personality—to make it clear what the store stands for, and to determine who the customer is—you need exquisite and defining judgment. A top-flight fashion director can best achieve the balance that keeps the older customer and attract the younger customer. Over the years I have noticed that some retailers ask their wives for advice. I do not recommend this.*

~ *Asking customers, as well as professionals, their opinions of your efforts will give you some candid thoughts you may not have been aware of.*

Three Ingredients

LUCK, TIMING, AND AWARENESS are three powerful ingredients of success when they come together. Take advantage of this.

Lessons Learned

~ *A good idea, whether old or new, is a good idea. Going back to French couture to jump-start Bergdorf Goodman's fashion image worked beyond our fondest dreams. Fashion-conscious customers are always interested when the fashion press recognizes exciting ideas.*

~ *Tobe's comment many years ago, "Front page news is front page fashion," appropriately summarized the reintroduction of the French couture to Bergdorf Goodman.*

~ *First identify the ingredients required to complete your company's successful product mix. Then, procure the merchandise with determination and tenacity.*

~ *To build a business you have to know both who your present customer is, and who you want your new customer to be. After that, the objective is to decide what type of operation or service will satisfy them both.*

Italian Designers

FENDI AND THE ITALIAN fashion designers taught me one lesson—loud and clear. Knowing your customers and knowing what they want is the first step. Acquiring what they want is the next.

Lessons Learned

~ *When you're trying to revitalize a business, there is almost always something—a trend, product line, or expert—that has enough industry recognition to redefine your company's meaning for customers. As soon as you discover this critical element, it is imperative that you pull out all the stops to align your company with this new direction.*

The Missing Element

THIS LESSON IS CRITICAL to the success of any business. Many start-up companies never make it because they miss at least one critical element.

Lessons Learned

~ *Three things are required to create a successful business—fashion or otherwise:*
  1. *Is the concept correct for the business? As a corollary, what does the business stand for?*
  2. *Is the financing appropriate?*
  3. *Is the organization professional?*
  All three are required. Otherwise, the business will collapse like a house of cards.

~ *Successful business relationships are best developed when both parties understand and agree on their mutual objectives. Writing down these objectives will help to eliminate any misunderstanding.*

~ *If you believe what you are doing is right, stick to your guns. Successful results will overcome nearly all adversity.*

~ *A store or a restaurant, like a person, must have a personality. That personality must be geared to the customer you are trying to attract. Consistency, recognition, and/or good food are necessary, but are not the only key elements.*

The Value of Gold

GOOD FINANCIAL EXECUTIVES can be worth their weight in gold. However, it is important to carefully delineate their responsibilities. Financial executives brought about the elimination of salespeople, extended store hours, and self-service.

Lessons Learned

~ *Some executives tend to view a business from the expense reduction opportunities. Merchants view a business from its growth opportunities. Both are right. However, it becomes a matter of not putting the cart before the horse. A merchant's responsibility is to build sales profitably. Financial people should manage expenses in order to grow the profit of the business. But without sales growth there will be no additional expenses to manage.*

Positive Thinking

POSITIVE THINKING MUST be followed by action. Otherwise the people involved will know it is only conversation.

Lessons Learned

~ *When a company makes a strategic decision, it is critical that all concerned—executives employees, suppliers, customers, and the press—be given the positive reasons for the decision. Otherwise negative thinking can snowball. Sometimes selling the positive is like pushing water uphill. But the positive must prevail.*

~ *"Build a better mousetrap" and "build a great baseball team and they will come," are not empty phrases. If a business's management stresses service and uniqueness, and maintains a complete and broad assortment of whatever is to be sold, the business will be a success.*

Showmanship

OUR STRATEGY OF BACKING UP initial promotions with the proper, dramatic designer shops attracted even more fashion designers and customers to Bergdorf Goodman. This can only be done when it is clear who the customer is and what the appropriate price level is.

Lessons Learned

~ *Retailing requires showmanship. No matter what type of store, customers and the press relate to drama and presentation. Fashion-interested customers do not need "new clothes," but they do need clothes that cause exciting feelings and conversation.*

~ *The press has always been and always will be helpful to those merchants who show creative merchandising and business ability. On the other hand, the press can do much harm to a retailer that appears not to be holding on to and building its share of the market.*

~ *When you are deciding a marketing strategy, it is imperative to know who your customer was, is, and will be. Equally as important is to know what type of environment this customer feels comfortable in? (This applies to fashion stores as well as department and discount stores.) Who the future customer will be is most important, since the future is now.*

~ *Bergdorf Goodman's new "European" second floor, which realized a rapid growth of sales and profit, was a high-profile reason that Carter Hawley Hale could claim that the capital budget invested in Bergdorf Goodman on Fifth Avenue was one of the best retail investments ever made.*

~ *Fashion, like any other business, has its stars. It is important to be able to identify the present leaders, but it is even more important to find the new talent before the competition does.*

~ *You have a tremendous competitive advantage if you can arrange to have the best merchandise lines exclusive to your store or business. Today the designers' distribution strategies make this approach almost impossible. However, it can still be done if you structure exclusive arrangements that will benefit the designer as well.*

~ *Nothing is forever. Marketing is always in a state of change. A retailer or designer can only maintain customer acceptance and loyalty by creating the merchandise, the image, and the environment that stimulates the customer in order to satisfy his or her desires.*

~ *Short-range planning will help to keep you in business a short time. Long-range planning will keep you there much longer.*

Fashion Soldiers

BERGDORF GOODMAN'S FASHION office decided which fashion collections the store would carry. Many retailers leave that decision to the buyers. Too bad.

Buyers are like soldiers. They must be directed. Left on their own, many will be successful. But many others will be casualties.

Lessons Learned

~ *The store's fashion directors know, before the buyers do, who the new successes are or will be. It is the function of the buyer to make the designer selected by the fashion office a merchandising success. It is not the function of the fashion office to enhance the prestige of a buyer's selection of a "safe designer's collection."*

Profitability

PROFITABILITY IS THE NAME of the game for everyone involved. Never, ever forget this.

Years ago, there were people who said that you can never make money in high fashion or expensive merchandise. Bergdorf Goodman became one of the most profitable stores in retailing. Other fashion stores and designers have since proved that there are fortunes to be made in luxury retailing.

Lessons Learned

~ *Good press will speed a talented designer on to success. Bad press will speed a mediocre designer on to his or her demise.*

~ *In retailing, as in other businesses, productivity is the key to success. High sales and gross margin productivity will bring a good merchant great success. Low productivity will always, eventually bring failure.*

~ *In the fashion business, it is just as important to have the best talent available for fashion guidance, as it is to have the best financial, operational, and merchandising guidance.*

~ *The merchandise division must recognize that the head of the company makes the key decisions to support the fashion executives. It is not for the people in merchandising to decide that they don't require guidance, and they can do just as well on their own. Those who feel they can do as well on their own should be let go to do just that.*

No Magic Formula

GOOD RETAIL ADVERTISING—newspaper, digital, or otherwise—attracts customers. Bad advertising will send a retailer to his or her demise. There is no magic formula for success. The principal of the business must know who his desired customers are, and how to reach them.

Lessons Learned

~ *As war is an extension of politics, advertising is an extension of merchandising. No advertising campaign is worth its salt unless it reflects sound merchandising strategy, policy, and concepts.*

~ *The fashion customer is always interested in something new. Designer names are exciting news to this customer.*

Competition

COMPETITION IS THE LIFEBLOOD of the retail business. It is not possible to know too much about your competitors. The strategy is always to attract their customers away from them to you.

Lessons Learned

~ *Fashion retailers should not only promote new designers, they should financially invest in them, so they can monitor their distribution and benefit from their licensing revenues.*

~ *Never be satisfied with your progress. There is always another idea, different from your competitor's. Competition is a threat to your business success. Study your competitors carefully, and fight them aggressively.*

~ *In the retail fashion business, it is as imperative to have a knowledgeable fashion director and an imaginative publicity director, as it is to have "a nose" in the perfume business. Both perform unique functions that are indispensible to success.*

~ *The principal of a retail business who wants his or her establishment to be a dominant fashion force must realize that a professional fashion director is as important as a newspaper editor, financial director, or operating officer.*

~ *No matter what business, the basic principles that successful executives have proven sound will, more times than not, lead to success.*

Stealing Their Business

SUCCESSFUL COMPETITORS HAVE USUALLY figured out the necessary steps to becoming industry leaders. This was true for Henri Bendel, across the street from Bergdorf Goodman, as well as for Bloomingdale's, a few blocks away.

The expression "steal their business" may not sound "professional" or much like a marketing strategy, but it is what Bergdorf Goodman had to do to become a dominant force in the fashion industry.

Lessons Learned

~ *Ownership will, more times than not, determine the future direction or demise of a business. Example: Federated Department Stores (Campeau Corporation).*

~ *Retail stores, like human beings, go through various stages of life. Some achieve success and high profiles, and then eventually pass on to oblivion in what would be considered a lifetime. A few go on, it seems, forever.*

The corporate entity that owns, and operates the stores is critical to which strategy and direction the store will take.

I often compare the heads of stores to ship captains. It is the skill with which the chief executives guides his stores through rough weather—and his keen understanding of the importance of basic retail fundamentals and principles—that determines whether or not his company eventually winds up on the rocks.

~ Customers, no matter what age or gender, and in good times or bad, are always looking for something new to make their lives a bit more exciting,

It has ever been thus and will continue to be, since fashion-conscious customers are always looking to enhance their lives and make them more glamorous. Business people must always recognize that the customer is looking to satisfy his or her desires. Otherwise their businesses will never achieve the great success that is available to them.

~ If you are to be successful in the luxury fashion business, customers must feel that they are being sold the newest and most exciting merchandise available.

Good luck and timing often help you achieve this objective.

The Best Teachers

MANAGEMENT BY WALKING AROUND (MBWA) and talking to salespeople—mine as well as my competitors'—taught me more than anything else about my business. What I learned about my competition was a bonus.

Lessons Learned

~ *A sound and imaginative marketing strategy for a business to grow to its potential is the first important step. It is critical to have a professional and talented organization, no matter how large or small, and specific direction from the company's objectives.*

~ *When a business has lost its position of leadership in any industry, it is imperative for that business to change direction in order to capture the attention of lost customers, as well as to attract a new audience.*

Fashion Shows

FASHION SHOWS ARE HELD for many different reasons. The best reason to stage a fashion show is to generate high-profile public relations.

Lessons Learned

~ *Customers interested in luxury merchandise can tell the difference between a fashion show staged for public relations and a fashion show geared to serious business. Comparison of sales generated by each type of event proves this.*

~ *As everyone undoubtedly knows, in any social event, charitable or otherwise, it is necessary to not only feature important business and social people as guests or sponsors, but also to include high-profile fashion designers and theatrical stars. This is a proven formula for success.*

Observe Talent

RETAILING IS ABOUT PEOPLE. From my first job opening doors for customers to becoming CEO, I found meeting, watching, and learning from people, at every stop along the way, was essential to understanding successful retailing.

Early in may career, I was fortunate to meet fashion designers as talented as Geoffrey Beene. Later, I had the good fortune to meet many other great designers—Michael Kors, Armani, and Yves Saint Laurent, to name just a few.

Lessons Learned

~ *Observe the talented, ambitious people around you. There is often a future star out there, waiting to be discovered. It might be you.*

~ *Enjoy good friendships. They don't last forever.*

~ *Since it is the fashion retailer's function to bring the newest and most exciting merchandise to its customers, experienced and professional buyers should, as they usually do, write their orders in the designer's showroom—quietly before or after all the fashion show hoopla for the press and for the crowd.*

~ *It was my good fortune was to be associated with successful, high-end luxury retailers—starting with my early introduction to Bonwit Teller & Co., at a young and impressionable age, and continuing throughout my business career. Aiming for excellence from the beginning, wherever you start, will always bring its rewards.*

~ *Being able to recognize talent, in designers and others, is a gift. If used wisely, it can bring great rewards to all concerned.*

   Being recognized requires the ability to demonstrate your talent in a manner that will make the powers that be aware of your future potential.

Excellence

MEETING PEOPLE LIKE Estée Lauder, Stanley Marcus, and Beatrice Fox Auerbach was inspiring. Each of them shared a desire for excellence that greatly contributed to my understanding of what it would take for Bergdorf Goodman to be a success.

Lessons Learned

> ~ *In every company, large and small, you will have the opportunity to form business relationships with other companies led by outstanding executives with inspirational qualities.*
>
> *It is important to identify these people. Slowly, but surely, let them become aware of your interest in their accomplishments and of your own ambitions.*

Customers Are Smart

THE FOLLOWING LESSONS ARE VARIED, but they all have one important theme in common: Customers are very smart. They almost always know what they want. I was fortunate enough to learn this early on.

I also learned from my competitors' mistakes. Some retailers expanded too rapidly. Others decided that a sale every day was an answer to generating higher profits. Others eliminated salespeople.

I found that Marshall Field had stated the most successful strategies many years ago. "Give the lady what she wants," he said. And, he added, "The customer is always right."

Lessons Learned

~ *Nearly every retailer, many still in business and some recently departed has at some point realized, sometimes, finally, when it was too late, that it has over-expanded. In the process, some of those retailers over-inventoried to the point of financial disaster—in some cases worse than that of The Great Depression.*

Many retailers, eager to reduce their expenses, make the cataclysmic error of drastically reducing their salespeople to the point that customers are left to look in vain for a sales person to make a sale. Example: Circuit City.

~ *If you want to reach your audience in the most positive terms, it is important to ensure that you are publicly associated and featured with the leaders of your field of endeavor. Good public relations will move a business on to success. Bad or negative public relations will help lead to its demise.*

~ *The great merchants taught me that the best way to attract customers into a store is to offer new and exciting merchandise every day of the year—or if not everyday, than as often as possible.*

Markdown and clearance merchandise should be the smallest part of the store's daily offering. This merchandise should be moved quickly—with the least advertising and the greatest markdown necessary to accomplish that objective.

~ *I repeat: Good advertising will speed a good merchant on to success. Good advertising will speed a poor merchant on to his demise.*

~ *As American retailers continue to expand nationally and even internationally, customer loyalty must be built into stores just as surely as bricks and mortar. It cannot be added as an after thought.*

Online retailers are slowly but surely developing a sensitivity to customer loyalty. This can be enough to make the average young customer gravitate away from brick-and-mortar retailers who think self-service is the answer to building a successful business.

~ Shopping is a very personal experience. Customers must be treated as valued assets—as individuals who require the store's attention and interest in their shopping needs. They should not be treated as a crowd of people who, if they look hard enough, may find what they want to buy.

The Men's Store

WHEN BERGDORF GOODMAN'S new men's store opened at the beginning of the 1991 recession, it did not reach its initial sales goal. The powers that be hired a focus group company that offered to pay each participant $100 for his input.

They failed to realize and to appreciate that the average customer for the men's store would think it normal to leave that much of a tip at a high-end restaurant. After the recession, the men's store achieved great success by adhering to the initial concepts. It was conceived as a store for the man whose wife shops at Bergdorf Goodman and who appreciates great quality and luxury.

Lessons Learned

~ *In any business, it is imperative to know as much as possible about your present and potential customer. Focus groups, like political pollsters, must ask the right people the right questions in order to get the right answers. Otherwise they generate the wrong answers and simply add to the confusion. The focus group should be your own customers. They, more than anyone, know what they like about your business and what it is they don't like.*

~ Customers are human beings and appreciate being helped. This can mean showing them where the merchandise they are looking for is located, or explaining what it will do for them. Anything that helps to makes the customer's shopping experience enjoyable will prove to be profitable. This is a much better strategy than hoping for good weather.

~ During any economic uncertainty, high-income customers will continue to purchase luxury merchandise in an elegant environment. Lower-income (aspiring) customers will drop out of the luxury market until the economy recovers.

~ "Give the customer what he or she wants," should be the touchstone for all salespeople, at all levels of retailing. Unfortunately, too many retailers today were not brought up knowing the importance of the productivity that professional salespeople can contribute. This lack of understanding has caused untold millions and millions of dollars never to be spent in their stores.

PUBLIC RELATIONS

CEO of Bergdorf Goodman

WHEN I TOOK OVER AS CEO of Bergdorf Goodman, my interviews with *The New York Times* and *Women's Wear Daily* were a bit sensitive, since the Goodman family had run the store for so many years.

In the same way, attending a Halston fashion show, when none of the attendees knew that I would be announced as Bergdorf Goodman's new CEO the next day, felt a bit dicey—especially given the sensitivities of this crowd.

Lessons Learned

~ *When you are required to talk to the press, be as positive as possible about whatever the subject is.*

~ *When a photographer is present, face the camera.*

The Press

WHEN I BECAME INVOLVED with the press, I treated reporters as partners. They helped me build Bergdorf Goodman's reputation for fashion leadership.

Lessons Learned

~ *Newspapers, like all businesses, have knowledgeable and ambitious people. If you help them they will help you. Helping does not mean leaking confidential information. They may consider this a favor, but it doesn't garner respect.*

~ *Unless the story is of major importance, give it to the newspaper that will best reach your audience. The caveat here is to be sure you explain this to the newspaper that didn't get the story first. Assure them that you will make up for it the next time.*

~ *Releasing the same story to all the press at one time may be safe, beneficial, and diplomatic, but newspapers, like all businesses, want to be first. You must select the medium that best serves your market.*

Credibility

Never, ever tell your employees one set of facts about your company's strategy and then give the press another. Your credibility will be destroyed.

Lessons Learned

- *When a company makes a strategic decision, it is critical that all concerned—executives employees, suppliers, customers, and the press—be given the positive reasons for the decision. Otherwise negative thinking can snowball. Sometimes selling the positive is like pushing water uphill. But the positive must prevail.*

- *Formal press interviews are geared to presenting the facts. The people giving the interview should always try to put a positive spin on the discussion. Sometimes, a picture speaks a thousand words*

- *Whatever the type of business, the press—the fashion press, entertainment press, etc.—is always looking for new products and new concepts or ideas to interest and stimulate their readers.*

It is critical to recognize which reporter, from which publication, is sympathetic, supportive, and very interested in your business concept or model.

~ Never forget that the press can make you or break you. The press can do you and your business a lot of good, but only if you treat it as a partner in your endeavors. Do otherwise at your own peril.

~ I repeat: Good advertising will speed a good merchant on to success. Good advertising will speed a poor merchant on to his demise.